There Are Many Ways

Poems New and Revised

To Pete Pagerow Wolanski
All the very best.
Enjoy!
Pete Trowes

www.hushdata.com/petetrower
www.harbour.com/petetrower
www.ekstasiseditions.com/petetrower

There Are Many Ways

Poems New and Revised

Peter Trower

Illustrations by
Jack Wise

Ekstasis  Editions

National Library of Canada Cataloguing in Publication Data

Trower, Peter
There are many ways

Poems.
ISBN 1-894800-05-2

I. Wise, Jack, 1928-1996. II. Title.
PS8589.R694T43 2002   C811'.54   C2002-910334-7
PR9199.3.T68T43 2002

© 2002, Peter Trower
Cover and text illustrations: Jack Wise
Cover design: Miles Lowry

Acknowledgements:
    Some of these poems have previously appeared in the following books: *The Sliding Back Hills, Bush Poems, Hitting the Bricks, Where Roads Lead* and *Chainsaws in the Cathedral.*

Ekstasis Editions Canada Ltd.   Ekstasis Editions
Box 8474, Main Postal Outlet   Box 571
Victoria, B.C. V8W 3S1   Banff, Alberta T0L 0C0

There are many ways has been published with the assistance of grants from the Canada Council and the Cultural Services Branch of British Columbia.

Contents

Author's Prologue   7
Upwind from Yesterday   11

Roots
Exhibits   15
The Only Deaths   16
Rebel on the Roof   17
When the Mill Was Our Mother   18
Thunderstorm   19
Little Red Schoolhouse   21
Old Man of the Mountain   24
Rainy My River   25
The Cargo Hulks   27
Brawls   29
Duchess   31
God Looks Out for Drunkards and Fools   33
Pulp Mill   35
Darkmountain Country   36

Coastlines
Where Roads Lead   41
Moon Song   44
Sea Cavalcade   45
Off Season   47
Driftwood   48
The Girls in the Froggy Mountain   50
The Dams and the Dynamos   52
Skookumchuck Solstice   53
Writer's Block on Soames Hill   54
Two Figments in January   56
Garden Music   57
Second Skeleton   58
The January Meadow   60
The Outer Island   61
The Storm Riders   62
Deep Places; Dark Places   64

Windworld	66
Longshoreman	67
The Dog	68
Skeletons	69
There are Many Ways	71
What the Wind Knew	72
The Abandonment	74
Kitimat Floor Show	77
Mohawk Jimmy	78
Thin Edge	79
Provisioning For a Long Journey	81

Inklings

Inklings	85
The Blasted Zone	87
Darks and Lights	88
Arctic Air Front	89
Prisons	91
Goodbye to the South	93
Decimal Street	95
The Falling Away	97
The Defector	99
Mars Probe	100
We Who Evade	102
The Day the Seas Went	104
Mansion	106
Sifting the Debris	108
My Thoughts Swim After You	111
On Uncharted Seas	113
Sweet Daddy in the Dark	114
Millenium	115
Remembering Al	117
Through the Apricot Air	120
The Pause	121

About the Author	123
About the Artist	124

Author's Prologue

This book has a convoluted history. It was originally intended as a sort of sequel to my first published poetry collection *Moving Through the Mystery,* illustrated by the remarkable artist, Jack Wise. Working with Jack was such an exciting experience, I wanted to repeat it as soon as possible. Unwisely, I threw together a second manuscript under the present title, that Jack illustrated for me in Spain.

I soon came to the uncomfortable realization that most of the poems were not up to the quality of the dazzling pictures. I worked for a couple of years, trying to improve the manuscript with new and better poems. Then I submitted to a couple of major publishers. After the second rejection, I could see that the book still fell short. I put it aside and went on to other endeavours.

Over the years, I wrote and published many other books but *There Are Many Ways* continued to elude me. Every so often, I returned to it and tried to beef up the contents. Nothing seemed to work. For a long time, I more or less abandoned the project, feeling very guilty at having let Jack down.

In the early Nineties, I began writing novels and my poetry production dropped off. A few good ones continued to materialize however and at length I put together another manuscript. I realized that this, finally, was the right vehicle for Jack's masterful drawings. So here they are in suitable company at last. Better late than never.

Peter Trower
Gibsons, B.C.
1998

There Are Many Ways

Upwind From Yesterday

Times that burned with pain and beauty
a chaos of friendships and disasters
moments that collapsed like imploded buildings
chances that flickered by and passed
the bitter sound of lost laughter

Upwind from yesterday
the shape of things alters and twists
The hurts diminish
The misapprehensions pack their bags
We are left with the trembling gist

A thousand foolish experiences
have scarred me   left me little wiser
I am a bemused atavist
in a present I barely understand
banging an obsolete typewriter

These are my passage-rites   my poems
I pass them to you come what may
I offer no apologies   no excuses
They are only residual echoes I have sifted
upwind from yesterday

Roots

Exhibits

The part of my heart still sliding
down a breathcaught hill
through the tobogganing twilight
in the lost cold warm to the memory
is the part of my heart still skating
across flooded Oxfordshire fields
before the war and the squandering
in the memory warm to the cold

Winters before comprehension
when my most signal terrors
were of ghostly footsteps in night-shrouded halls
the scorn of my small shrill peers
Days of naive expectation
exploded in Guy Fawkes excitement
as laughing in bonfire-lit innocence
we roasted our ritual traitor

And having learned of paternal death
like an unbelievable rumour
I found summer apples on stable shelves
wrinkled but still tart-sweet
munched them in tingling ignorance
doubting my father's fatality
certain he'd hero home someday
his arms full of trophies and answers

The apples rotted to blue dust
my father never came back
and when the war drums hammered
we fled that world in the bomb-haunted dawn
Now in a faded English dream
I move through museum distances
touching the dim diminished exhibits—
the shapes of my past—remotely

The Only Deaths

The only deaths that count are the deaths of others
naive illusion falls away from our faces
leaving them naked and open, the guile gone
an indefinable knowledge about the eyes

My father was half my age, the day he died
crushed in a broken plane and our futures altered
above his doom's red minute, a bird sang
and snow lay white and chill on his lost mountains

The only deaths that count are the deaths of others
the nullified need blink no further tears
under the ultimate anaesthetic, they enter totality
rejoin the mysterious whole, forgetting their lives

It is the burden of the quick to touch the small voids
the dead leave   the discomforting quiets
to ponder the assassin in the grass blade
the executioner in the rose petal

Beginning stumbles into end   the pattern is random
or it is not random   meaningful or without meaning
the solution is everywhere   or it is nowhere
we are inept detectives forever tracking red herrings

This way has been walked before   there are many lies
few truths   the world is its own garbled answer
the only deaths that count are the deaths of others
and naive illusion falls away from our faces

Rebel on the Roof

Incorrigible schoolmate
you crouch yet on the sloping slates of memory
far above our envious eyes—
the angry commands of masters
in that most-staid of British prep-schools
obedient to clocks in scholarly Oxford—
most spectacular of rule-flouters
tiny with breathless triumph against the sky

So few dared to be rebels then
in those ordered halls of early learning
that your image stands like a symbol
still undimmed by recollection
Of course you were summarily expelled
for that singular act of defiance—
went on to become a steeplejack   an actor
or a successful politician

Now in a time of many rebels
when the streets are raucous with dissent
the status quo quivers under assault
and the old belief systems are crumbling at last,
I think of that boy with the forgotten name
clinging stubbornly to those steep tiles
They shout change wholesale from the rooftops of today—
are far too numerous to expel.

When the Mill Was Our Mother

It dreams on in green memory
that small shabby outport
jammed between woods and water
in a sun-forsaken place
where life proceeded slowly
to the mill's growling edicts—
where time was kept by whistles
below the hooded mountain's face

When the mill was our mother
orchestrating the days—
an erratic-tempered mother
of timber, brick and rank smells—
an uncouth mother
of belching stacks and old machinery—
a strict-minded mother
bending us surely to her will

Yet, a nurturing mother
who deeded us a town to live in
tumbledown   without pretensions
on the rainy river's brink
full of tarpaper palaces
with pulp-lined interiors—
full of simple caring people—
full of truth and common strength

Like one family we lived
in the lost times   the unforgotten times
in the lean times   the rough and ready times
that were not like any other
In that kingdom of friendly destiny
we had nothing   we had everything
by the tossing seas of silver yesterday
when the mill was our mother

Thunderstorm

The thunderstorm
came crackling   gnashing and rumbling
out of the Squamish Valley
down-inlet towards us
on a myth-stricken night
when I was too young to know terror
and lived in a limberlost house
beside the moribund mill
that loomed like a haunted palace
with its Poe-touched roof-rims and towers
its bankrupt ghosts   its silences
while beyond in the crowded black forest
bears lumbered and snuffled
birds slept wise in their high-rise nests
slugs slime-trailed across the woods' floor
hunting owls haunted the trees
and the wilderness clawed at our shaky toe-hold

The thunderstorm
came tumbling   twitching and crashing
closing in on us like a war
spasming light through my bedroom window
shaking the peaks with its judgement-day voice
breaking the peace in that peace-rich place
rattling the tall doors of childhood
But I felt no fear
of those midnight pyrotechnics—
those bolts   explosions   rambunctions
Simple naivete held me invulnerable—
safe from the storm's thumping fury

The thunderstorm
cannons off into distant memory   Today
when the sky explodes, I know better
than to feel exempt from its anger
for I
have been struck by lightning
have felt
the sledgehammer force of it
have tasted
its life-cancelling power and I know
the sabres that slash from the clouds
play no favourites

Little Red Schoolhouse

Gabriella, my dear woman
whatever possessed you
to become a schoolmarm
in the first place?

Sour Gabriella
with your unkissed spinster face
imposing almost insoluble math problems on us
for minor offenses

But we fooled you, Gabriella—
sneaked down to the mill office—
had the problems solved by sympathetic secretaries
on the company comptometer

And one day, Gabriella
before we learned that dodge
I fell deliberately into a winter stream
on the way to school—
ran home   pleaded pneumonia
spent two days in bed
rather than face emptyhanded
your petulant wrath

How we dreaded you, Gabriella
with your highstrung mannerisms—
your squeaky peevish voice

So it must have been some sort of poetic justice when
while haranguing the class one morning,
the elastic in your knitted skirt broke
and it dropped to the floor
revealing skinny unshaved legs in lisle stockings
old-fashioned bloomers
to our incredulous eyes

You ran hysterically from the room, Gabriella
your authority destroyed—
tendered your resignation   left town on the next boat

I wish all my ogres
had thrown in the towel
as easily as you.

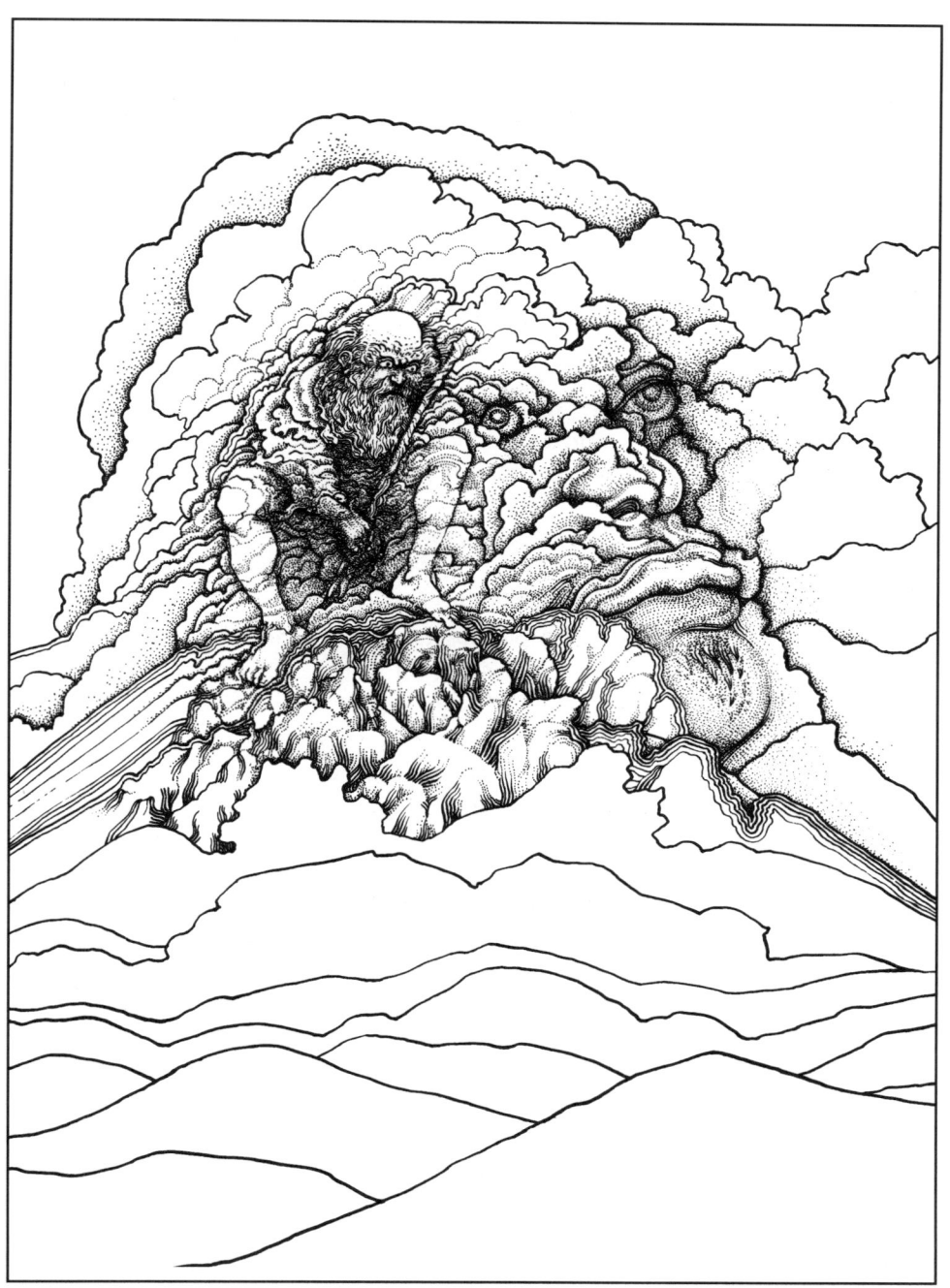

The Old Man of the Mountain

The old man of the mountain
gnarled myth of my youth
squints through a cloud window
from his wind-haunted roost
He is waiting there yet
on that boy-visioned peak—
wiser than sanity—
more real than rain—
wrinkled and storm-bearded
with all-seeing eyes
and a knobby walking staff
to shake at the stars

The cynics of maturity
dismissed his heady legend—
banished him scornfully
to the simple closets of childhood
But he will be returning
on a day with a final number—
the cinders of lost fantasy
will kindle to glowing fact—
he will drift down through the ceiling
at my life's ultimate instant—
I will greet him resignedly   sadly
my poem-father of dreams.

Rainy My River

Rainy my river
and constant my valley,
vibrant with memories
castle your mountains
round the greenpurple
and brown of your floorland
new-timbered bottomland
bright in the sunsplash
snag-fingered bottomland
flame-blackened phantoms
shades of that holocaust
fire of the Forties

Rainy my river
still tirelessly roaring
down from the glacial
womb of your birthplace
crystalline blood
for the veins of a pulpmill
crystalline drink
for the taps of the thirsty
cradle of fish
for the lines of the leisured
white-whiskered waterman
running your rockroad

Rainy my river
tumultuous   timeless
mirror of entropy
prisoning moments
loggers and shakecutters
hikers and hunters
schoolboy adventurers
fleeing from bear-fear
self-absorbed lovers
adream on your pathways
whirl them all down
to the answerless ocean

Rainy my river
and constant my valley
where I again
have invaded your borders
stand in caulk-boots
on resonant ridges
sweating and cursing
and stealing your timber
writing your poems
and guilty of living
constant old valley
and rainy old river

The Cargo Hulks

Ramshackle barges
limp the coastal passages
carrying hogfuel and sulphur
to the ever-hungry mills—
food for the insatiable
bellies of the digesters—
ammunition for the smokestacks
to vomit at the gulls

Cargo hulks
stripped of masts and superstructure—
name   rank   indentity—
any vestige of esteem,
they flounder through the waves
like great gutted whales
behind the strutting tug-boats
and they dream

of full sail—
ferocious high seas thundering—
merciless antarctic gales—
the howling challenge of the Horn—
shrouds under full stress bulging
like a trumpet player's cheeks—
the pitching   the nearly foundering
the forging on

to dolphin country
in the long rolling heat
past stark coasts where volcanoes growl
like old men in beds—
equatorial becalmings—
deckboards cracking in the sun—
parched voices croaking for a wind
on the hard green road

Blowing north again
before a good kicking gust
through starhung climbing nights
and new-minted days
to drop anchor at last
winner of the harrowing marathon
before new-raised cabins smoking wlecome
in the pioneer bays

Memories melting
in the cold reality of the rain
they wake to ultimate winters by wharves
in the overwhelming stink
become mere pawns
in the same industrial equation
that fouls the water brown and foaming
along their flanks.

Brawls

Breathless with delight
we see the grade b western barrooms
erupt in the ersatz violence
of choreographed donnybrooks
balsawood chairs
splintering over hapless heads
candy windows smashing   the hero
swinging from handy chandeliers
to boot the badmen in the belly.

John Wayne and Randolph Scott
colliding like titans
trading merciless haymakers
each one enough to poleaxe an ox
yet up they jump unscathed
like tireless robots
to slug their way through klondike dancehalls
in fistic marathons that end
with the foregone *coup de grace*
and the slightly-mussed victor
reeling back to the bar
for a manly shot of cold tea.

Young Broderick Crawford
walloping adversaries
with great meaty mitts
in southsea honky tonks
Ward Bond's hulking renegade bully
challenged by slight Dana Andrews
grunting: "I'll get you, Logan!"
as a whiskey bottle breaks on his skull—
cocky James Cagney
toppling bullies twice his size
abandoning words for right hooks
in a backlot Hell's Kitchen—

William Bendix and Alan Ladd
battling side by side
an army of oriental thugs
in the alleys of a canvas Saigon.

How they tussle   tumble
toughtalk through our dreams
the named and nameless scufflers
of those bloodless set-tos
forgotten stuntmen of a sawdust universe
leaping valiantly from balconies
absorbing sometimes
more than imaginary punishment
for union scale
and the sake of our naive joy.

But one Saturday afternoon
in that boyhood pulpmill town
an old drunk comes to the matinee
to noisily annoy
the normally placid projectionist
until he loses control
drags the offender outside
administers a brutal battering
out of all proportion to his sins
leaves him lying there
like a sack of garbage
giving the lie to hollywood punch-ups
dribbling real-life unpretty gore
before our stunned and disillusioned eyes.

Duchess

She roared like an autumn gale
through the sober world of my childhood
with three unruly terriers
and bottles of scotch in her suitcase

The Irish eyes jigged bright
in that chipped patrician face
How I admired and feared her
shrill worldly remittance woman

Iernie, my renegade aunt
sent packing for stealing a ring
in the days when they swept such embarrassments
beneath the Colonial rug

It wasn't whiskey alone
that furrowed those elegant features
It was also years of loneliness
rejection and harrowing exile

She never wanted for money
till a gigolo bilked her for most of it—
she bought him fine clothes and a yacht—
he gave her only his treachery

Other exploiters laughed
and vied for the rest of her nest-egg
cruelly amused by the spectacle
of a tipsy toppled lady

Iernie became a legend—
a died-in-the-wool eccentric—
held court in upcoast shanties
with her dogs, cheap wine and memories

She misbehaved in the bars
when her monthly stipend arrived—
drank like a man with the men—
the locals called her "the Duchess"

But beneath the bawdy facade
she ached for her vanished lineage—
she brooded on family trees—
the kinfolk who had rejected her

A month before she died
I talked with my outcast aunt
She rambled about our ancestors
I felt the true weight of her pain

God Looks Out For Drunkards and Fools

After they'd bid me goodbye and good riddance
    I gunned the outboard and rattled away
       tight as a tick with four cases of beer
  the mountains wobbling up all around me

"You'll never make it!" I heard someone shout
    I wasn't all that sure I would either
    but I was too addled to give a goddamn
    hammering up the Sound in the sunlight

    The boat was a Salmon Derby prize
I'd bought from the winner the night before
Eight hundred hard-won bucks he soaked me
He'd had it a year   Perhaps I'd been robbed

But it floated and moved   that seemed sufficient
I voyaged through my fantasies steering it proud
    a vessel-possessor   King of the Inlet
my clinker-built cockleshell carving the waves

    Cracking more beers to befuddle my wits
I chug-a-lugged on from one town to another
      singing insane duets with the engine—
    the day unreeling and reeling around me

I was halfway there when the motor died
I cranked it like hell but it paid no attention
I found they'd neglected to give me the oars
   Mechanical moron, I cursed and drifted

     The Sound was empty of boats to hail
  I was far from shore and the sky was clouding
What if a storm should blow up?   I had nightmares
   of high winds lambasting me into oblivion

In panic, I worried the engine again—
yanked on the rope till I damn near fell overboard
and just when I'd come to the end of my hope
it coughed back to life and prodded me east

It was dusk when I docked at the Woodfibre mill
with a sigh of relief and most of my beer
Lugged it all up to the Sunday-dry bunkhouse—
rallied my buddies and drank half the night

Rattletrap boat of beer-swilling youth—
you lie long-sunken in Howe Sound silt
Vagabond vessel of haphazard years—
you drum through my dreams like a metaphor.

Pulp Mill

Stinking smoke haze
blurs
the bluegreen beyond
Tree flesh and chemicals
combine
to form a fecal sludge
a rough brown sheet
a bleached white sheet
a thin white sheet
this page

Birds choke through bitter winds
above concrete walls
where busy stacks belch
timeclocks click
circuits stutter
presses crush
cylinders rotate
reducing forests
to their essential fibres
the holy goal of product

Day and night
those nevertiring gears
grind out pollution
and paper
for books   bags   boxes
coloured toilet tissue
while in the natural factories
of the farther hills
fresh stands of timber
struggle industriously up
towards
industrial disaster.

Darkmountain Country

In the darkmountain country
the stump-house stands broken-windowed
the cabins are hammered to rubbish
the alders have taken the clearing
To our lost home by the milltown
the cat fled back and went feral
waited its tameness away
for footsteps that never came back

The pulp factory still vomits smoke
below the rain-making mountain—
brackish and bitter, the sea
sickens the fish with its poisons—
cranebuckets peck at the sawdust
with ravenous steel teeth—
the monster eats well as always
grinding the trees into money

The swing-bridge, a hammock of memories
spans the spring-busy river—
its boards have forgotten our feet
that trudged them times beyond counting
The pub it once led to is gone
a victim of change and expansion
We used to squander our pay there
when we'd traded our boyhoods for beer

There is no trace left of us now
in this place that was once life's centre—
scant proof that we ever existed
in the phased-out riverside town
Around us the past disappears
in a flurry of faces and voices—
sadly we turn from this shadowland,
ghosts of the rained-away years.

Coastlines

Where Roads Lead

Empty signboard nailed to a tree
like a face without features
gives me no directions   I
need none anyway   the day
draws me with warm hands
up this rough and vacant road
to rocky vantage points where others
have paused to gaze on stillwood gullies
watertanks and houses torn
from wilderness   no wind   the small
far hill I'd love to build
a castle on   the veinblue mountains
between   beyond, the sunflecked
spectrum of the sea

Turn to the brush   the lure
of the land urges me on
up branch roads leading
past abandoned homesteads
where only weeds keep watch now
to stand in the gutted shell of a house
that has lost its people
and sinks into the green tide of the bushes
with cobwebbed windows
and still a rusty lock on the door
where some hesitant hand
turned the key on yesterday

Today, I seek where roads lead
into my mind and out as I move them through me
and move along them and move
through the questioning day

But I know in my heart they are circular
twisting back on themselves like moebius strips
like tail-devouring snakes
In this roundabout riddle
there are no real destinations.

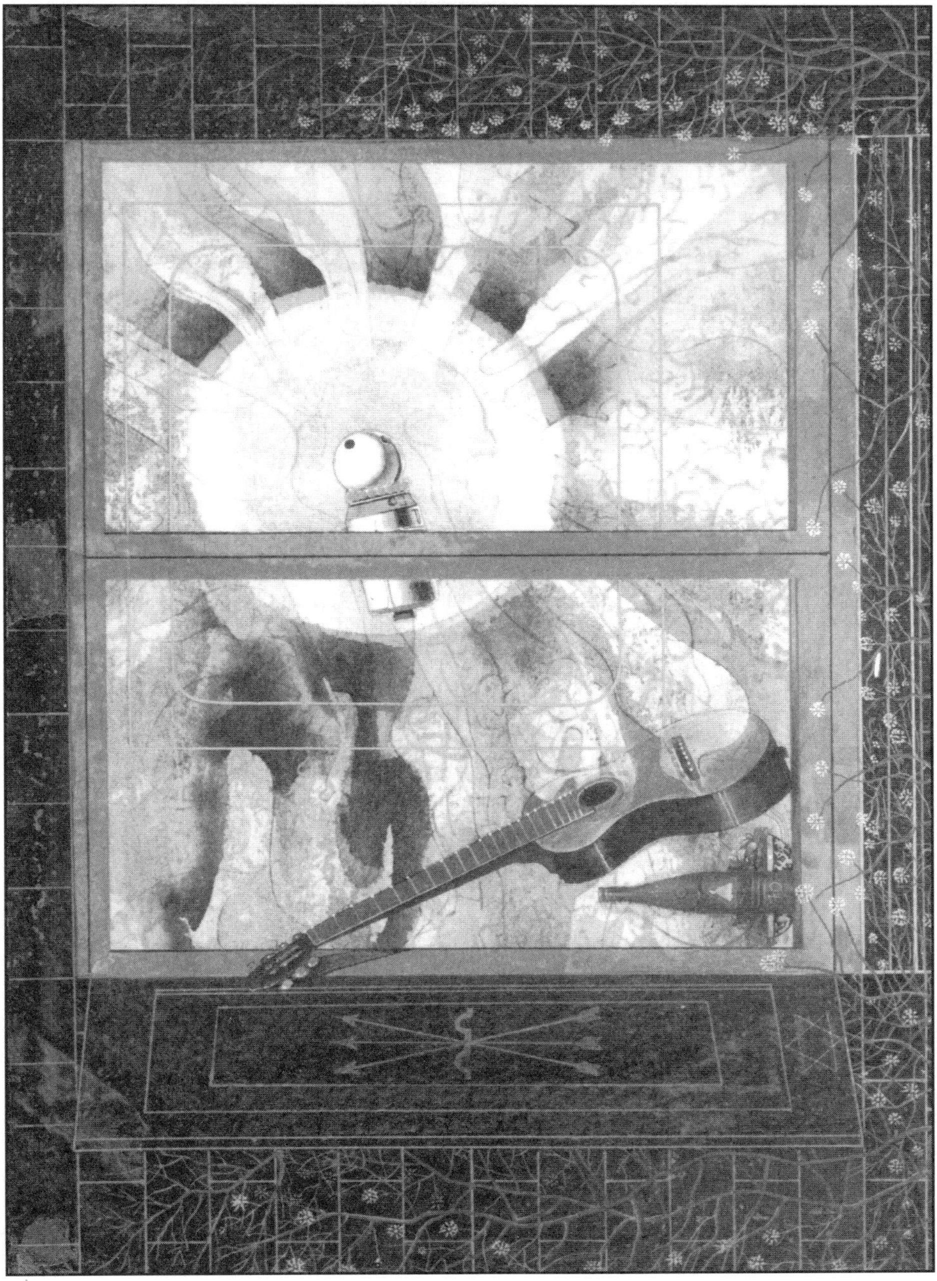

Moon Song

This night the world is mine and the moon's
peering like a lambent eye
through a porthole of pale cloud—
cratered globe of space-battered stone—
hypnotist's watch
unleashing madmen   awakening werewolves—
tugging the tide up like wet sheets—
you're open for business, ball of myths

Christmascard trees, black in your brittle light
backdrop my ramshackle hideaway—
you're a scarred yellow pool ball
cued and rolling forever across the night's table—
you're the pock-marked pusher
peddling dreams in dusk-clotted alleys—
I'll buy your wares, old brother—
anything's better than earthbound lies

You are my heart gone sick from the universe
raddled rock lantern of ungranted wishes—
sun-muscles twitch you golden—
we throb to the same dim principle
all birds   all trees   all beasts and people—
only God knows the rhyme or reason—
He lets you shimmer on like a beacon
and lets me shiver on like a fool

Sea Cavalcade

Through warm veins of day
the blood of the village taps
a holiday chorus of sirens, horns and drums
rises and falls between the amplified voices
They are having a parade
to celebrate tourists and summer money
Yesterday they blew up a schooner
with pirateblack sails
circled it in a fireboat as it sank
waving hosestreams like small boys with sticks

The procession winds on
along the streets of country August
slow congaline
of hooves, wheels and feet
moving inexorably
to disbandment point
dissolving there
in a grumble of children and following dogs

A delegation of talkative birds
fills a grandstand seat
on the skyraft
of a television antenna
swapping
southern advice and addresses
for the winter they feel in their wings

Against gilt clouds
on the higher road of the hill
the floats and figures of the trees
move yet
to the marching brass of the wind
celebrating
the greater occasion
that never ends

Off Season

In the manicured cove
like that secure ultimate harbour
no one ever reaches,
we uncover the dullbronze disc
of a moss-bearded cornerpost—
measure ramps and floats
for a suit of changes
as the sun falls down autumn airslopes
to the waterbeetle boats

It is a buttery day
spreading like a salve
over fresh abrasions
Brushed by wintergreen winds
we tug at our chains
in the late-morning dazzle
while two pudgy tycoons
phone San Francisco from a booth
and the jellyfish gesture diaphanously

In lethargic noon
we sit among the dreamghosts
of yearning vacationers
banished by summer's end
to tense identical suburbs
and we commiserate with them   we
who move unfairly in the fair places—
walk in changing wonder
the whole cartwheeling year.

Driftwood

That clawed-rooted wind-broken tree
battered down by God-knows-what wild river
over the flooding Sound
to fall across our garden bottom
like an exhausted traveller

Even the scavenging beachcombers
can find no worth in it
It has floundered here unwanted
on the bucking back of the tide
to sprawl haplessly across our doorstep

The forest has aborted it
flung it from the green womb
like a pried-free foetus
It is dead   gnarled   splintered   knotty
barkless as a bone

Until some high sucking sea
relaunches that travelsore wanderer
it will sentry our seagate like an omen
of forestdeath   mandeath
the endless mutability of things

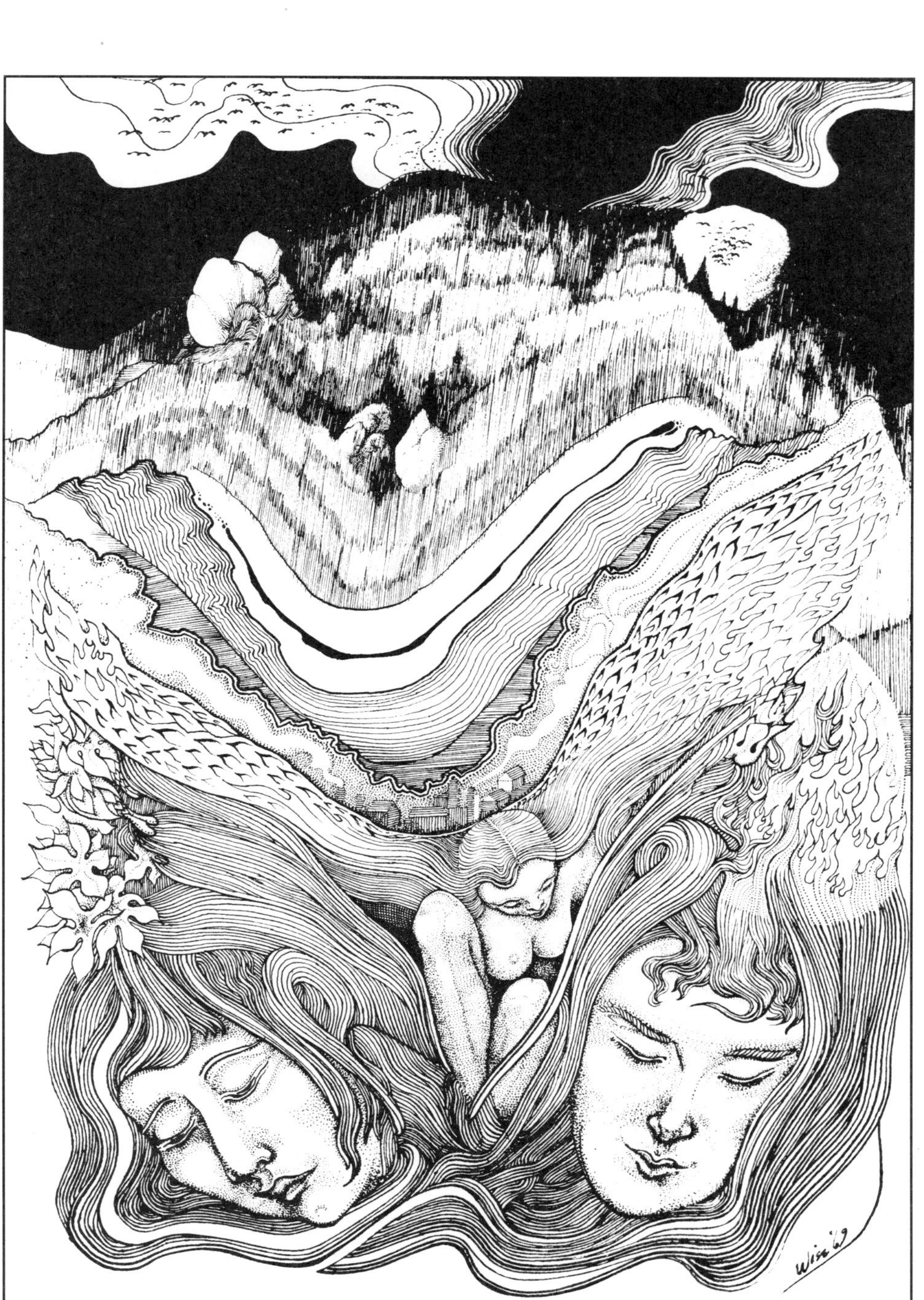
Wise '69

The Girls in the Froggy Mountain

A dark confetti of crows
clenches and spreads
across the pale tableau
of the January town
below the mountain squat as a frog
with its enigmatic smile
of tree-toothed logging slash

There was a time
in this methodical place
before rough machinery
carved out that mile-wide smirk
before intrusive buildings
elbowed back the forest
and hooked their eyes
to the television sky,
when the world proceeded
at an idler pace
and free-range cows wandered at will
along the blackberried roads

Then, coquettish with spring,
the girls walked wind-haired
down the schoolday hill
tempting our cracked and tongue-tied voices
with immemorial smiles—
sidling through our dreams
all the uneasy night

Until, in the slow arc of awakening,
we found the music of each other
walked hand in hand
the beaches of high summer
to kiss the evenings away

              The lovely   the lost
       they have danced their last home waltzes
           to the stardust trombones of time—
               they are fled forever
        from the dawnplays they were golden in

                Swollen with change
              the utterly-altered town
       sprawls across the stripped civilized slopes
          below the inscrutable froggy mountain
       that has swallowed the bright girls of morning

The Dams and the Dynamos

Until the poles and the powermen topple
there will be red energy under the eggs—
fireflies to fire the bulbs—
flickering ghosts in hypnotic boxes—
fans to tickle us cool—
thermostat heaters to wake us warm—
music plucked from the air—
until the dams and the dynamos break

We have become too at ease with ease—
we suck the lazy electric tit—
our homes are dependent husks
only bought lightning prickles alive
We hide in sizzling cities
with factories that conveyor us fat—
screens full of demon lovers—
shrewd computers that audit our souls

And when the cord severs sometimes
in truthblack winters in storms, we curse
through dark with the cold mounting
down to candles and uncertain batteries
If the outage persisted, we'd set
trueflames in our plastic fireplaces—
beg the atrophied knacks—
but always the power returns again

Until the dams and the dynamos break
we will hibernate in complacent caves
watching the lost of the world
shiver and die in swamp and desert
We will sorrow or simply shrug
the acknowledged children of affluence
till the lights go dead   for good
and thin hands smash through our privileged windows

Skookumchuck Solstice

The day is slack with heat
the sun leans on the leaves above us
we move along the path in cool shade

The waters are slack at this moment
they are mustering their energies
it is between rounds

Soon we sit among strangers on front-row decks
a last boat flees by
the sea begins to froth and trouble

A rising river of incoming tide
collides with the thrust of the outfall
the sea locks horns with itself

Waterquake   two behemoths arm wrestling
locked in titanic contest
elemental stalemate on the first day of summer

We have gathered for this clash of waters
in the sea gut between the gashed mountains
it is a ritual   a sort of homage

Writer's Block on Soames Hill

Beside you on the rim
of the moss-thatched summit
we have attained gasping
this evening of impulses,
I strain too hard for poetry
see only a village
sprawled in a crook of land
last sunlight splashing
golden from windows
to join in a giant jellyfish form
on the flat bay perhaps
some other whimsical time   tonight
only light
the mountains
only mountains
the boats
simply boats   no images   they won't
come when you try to force them
but lie dormant   things
are as they seem   no more

Later descending
that deadsteep trail
reflective among the bony trees
feeling old logger muscles
work in my legs
first time in years,
I clasp you when I can
kiss you when we clasp my
soft girl of strangenesses
whose defenses melt easily
to the proper heat
melt as we move
downmountain to the car

to whatever we must
perhaps a tender magic
better than the poem
I reached for to no avail
on eaglerocks with vistas
too vast for grasping.

Two Figments in January
(*The filming of* A Wild Girl)

On a day half dazzle   half fog
an eagle swims above weedy trees—
the sun explodes like a bomb—
the teeth of the wind are keen with winter
We are several snowfalls from spring—
the day is a two-faced coin—
the mist hangs thick on the earth's edge—
the rest: blue glisten   green candor

On a day half menace   half hope
I walk once more with a wild girl
through weathers and dreams of a different time
but the actress beside me is not my love
Over the stump wastes   among the trees
we seek to embellish the image—
honey and lemon this later sun—
fog on the rim of my heart like a weight

On a day half fancy   half fact
we rock in a flat-bottomed boat
into the shivering earth's-end mist
where time is frozen and no birds weave
By spidertree islands that ghost through the blur
we skirt the brink of the world
Churn back to sun from that chilly abyss
dark to light as our lives move.

Garden Music

Music in the garden—
pure cry of flowers—
I am ringed with wise colour—
August chords of tint
singing out to the universe—
one dark red Stravinski rose
magnificently conducting
golden horns of the marigolds—
harps of fleshpink phlox—
mauve cellos of the daisies—
reeds of purpleyellow pansies—
pastel violins of the fading hydrangeas

I hide from the heat
this orchestrated afternoon
crouching drowsy
in the shadecave of the dying summer lilacs—
the bony laburnum with its poisonous pods
thinking of a girl with sunwarm skin
I kissed before she left
and will kiss again—
who is part of the music of this day—
this throbbing dark beneath the bushes
where I listen to the garden playing
arrangements of the rocks and grass

Second Skeleton

Letter from a girl fallen
over the edge of herself
received on a pale day
when clouds have risen
like blister tissue
on the sunburned sky

Letter from a girl finished
with unmanagable realities
for a time of no telling—
given to sedated wards
where they will endeavour to untie
the hurting knots of anger

You have been with me in this garden
beside the cornmothers cradling
their ragdoll cobs
I have sensed
the pressure of your tension—
the twisted uglier part of you
beneath the pretty—
that symbiotic entity of dread and self-hate
who lives like a second skeleton
in all of us
thriving hungrily
on what we wish worst for ourselves—
battening on our frets and terrors

When you were last here
only your anguish held you upright
as the thin stakes shakily support
the tomato plants

I wanted somehow
to stroke your agonies calm—
to starve the entity of your hurt—
to soothe you with whatever love I know

But I too
carry a malignant passenger
Though I often try to drown him silent
he steers my cowardice like a ship

Letter from a girl gone searching
for help in a likelier direction
May the pain assuagers grant you
a few good secrets of peace

The January Meadow
For Larry Sealey

Yesterday was yes
to your fields of dappled horses
your extravagant plans emblazoning
the homestead's quiet ruin with hope
your sure enthused face
like a benign backwoodsman's in a myth
the utter inevitability
of your heady winterbright visions

Yesterday was yes
in the neglected fields
of the long-abandoned farm—
my mind echoed your enthusiasm
till I could almost see the Appaloosas
of your hoofbeat imagining
whinny and run
on that drained lake-floor of fine earth

Yesterday was yes
because it had to be—
there was no room for negative thought—
the trees spoke hope
In the forgotten clearing
beyond the reach of all skeptics
the afternoon exulted
and I smelled the musk of new life

The Outer Island

There were times when the water lathered and leapt
lurched and crashed through the gap
barring us from the island
We had tried it once when the weather frowned
bucked till we lost the prop
and wet white fingers drummed us back to the mainland

So we went there only on diamond days
when the sea arched soft to the sun
beached in a cove of tree chunks—
slashed our way through the braiding brush
to the hush of the island's heart—
traced our invisible lines between bluffs and tree-trunks

Through hoary jungles of high salal
we whittled with saw and knife,
the transit findings to mark us—
pounded plugs in the rain-pecked rock—
hammered stakes in the earth—
learned the land and carved it up like a carcass

In the last lax hours, we walked the shore—
sprayed our names on a cliff—
pictured the coming hordes of town-vacators
Our thoughts blew south on a cynic's wind—
we gunned the outboard for home
and left an island betrayed to the speculators

The Storm Riders

On an afternoon of storm
we stand at the window
watch the piling upset heavens
roil beyond the glass

Above the echo-swept mountains
great breakers of cloud
tumble and crash
against each other and the shores of the peaks

They rattle their anger at us
after each nerve-bright flash
like drummers gone mad with war
beating tattoos against the cannonlight

Black   vast   vaporous
creatures of storm-smoke
come twisting like dust-devils
across the middle distance

A stampede of birds
spills inland like a demoralized army
as their element turns ugly
above the gun-metal sea

Beyond the possessed sky
great hooves hammer dimly
four patient horsemen
are rehearsing Apocalypse

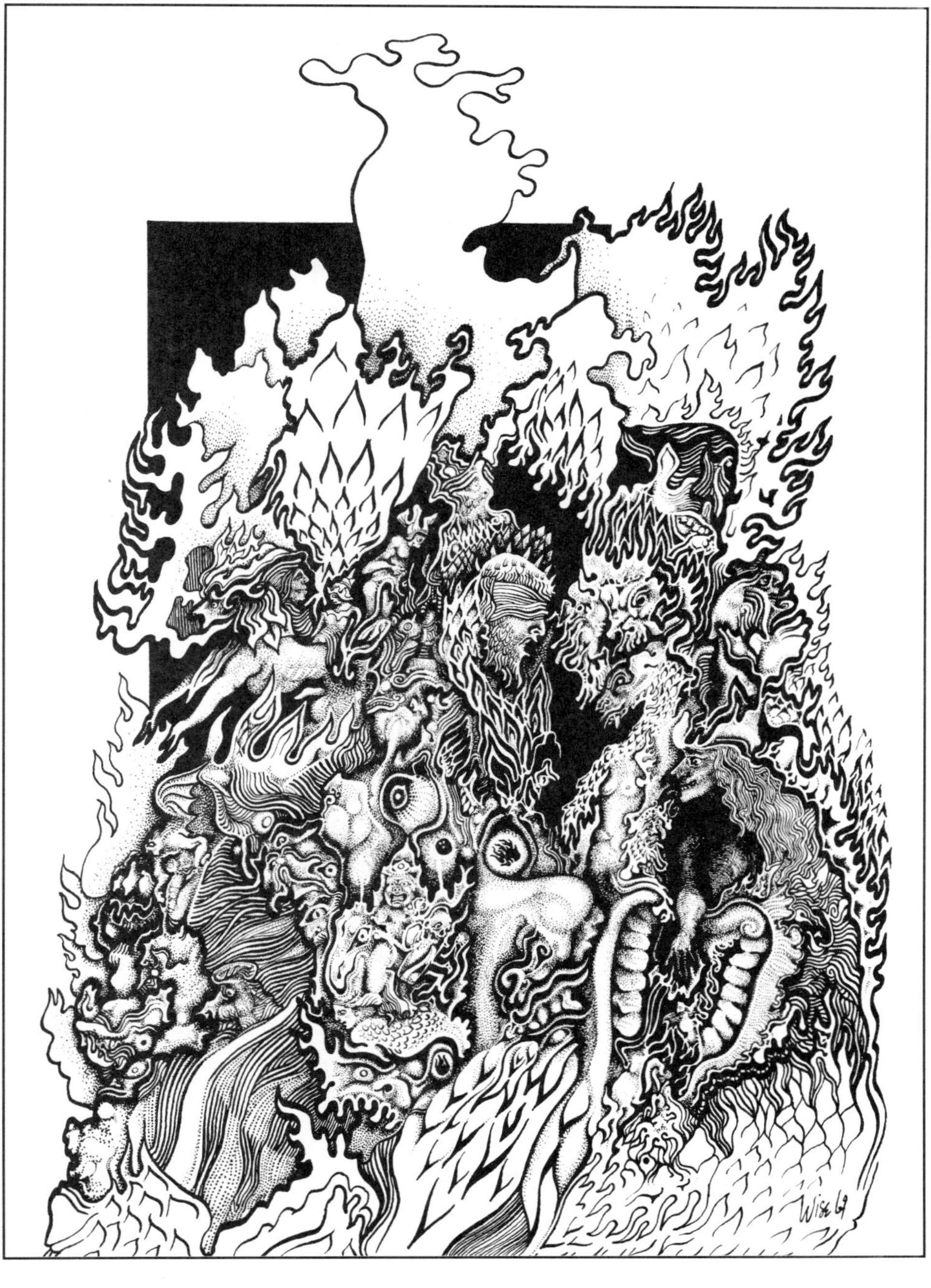

Deep Places; Dark Places

In the fist of the nightmare
the phantoms of my worst imaginings
taunt me with humourless laughter—
twisted implacable faces
leer at me in the ominous court
of Kafkaesque injustice
where they are passing
an unthinkable sentence on me
for unknown crimes

I scream at them in my own defence
to no avail—
the thing is done—
there are no appeals
I spit futile curses at them—
try to run—
wrestle desperately
with three faceless guards—
wake suddenly—
only I'm not awake
but trapped in the skewed and sinister
room-that-is-not-the-room
where every creak and rustle
is fraught with festering terror—
where the cat is a hissing demon
and grubwhite fingers
claw at me from the couchback

I fight my way upward
through the fathoms of the black dream—
it is harder that ever before
but I break through at last
to the dubious safety of the surface
lie there damply quivering—
knowing that one of these nasty nights
I'm not going to make it

Windworld

A wind cold as ghosts
rattles through dead bamboo
out of the talltale north
hisses from tombstone plateaus
into the mainsails of day

Some few birds fling
through the galloping tempest
giving hoarse joyful cries
of soaring acknowledgement

This is a country of unquiet skies
like chill thoughts
scrubbed so blue by winter
that even clouds
huddle behind the snowshocked peaks

Scoured by the wind
mountains rear naked shoulders
where loggers have sheared their pelts away
Old roads snake across them
like great walls of China
in battering January

The angry wind will die in time
and calm be reinstated
but for now, it rules unchallenged
strewing chaos in its wake
raising its rambunctious voice
howling down all opposition

Longshoreman
for Alex Will

That small articulate man
who was more alive than most
lay down by the Black Tusk trail—
in his sleep became the mountain
Six hikers carried him out
a burden beyond first aid
leaving his laughter there
bequeathed to the alpine summer

In the City, his docks toil on
for the waiting steam-bound ships
A new generation of hold-rats
banters to work on the waterfront
Somebody whispers his name
in the towers of wheat where the shovels clacked
and one-armed Charlie Chatter
taps out a ghost-hook salute

He's struck to the telling now
along with Siderunner Sid
Nannygoat   Coffee-an' Joe
Wimpy and Coalheaver Smith
There will be no more galley-slave holds
or terrible Terminal Docks—
he has battened his final hatch—
he has sweated his goodbye cargo

The Dog
for Ted and Marge Poole

Irrepressible exuberance
reefing at the leash—
four-legged helium balloon
whose *up* is straight on
through Ambleside Park
in the Bridge's broad shadow

Great buoyant boy of a dog
drunk with pure scent and feel
straining at his leash down the sea-path
past glum men gathering kelp scraps
and a pondful of wrangling ducks

Released, he bounds like a bandit
with a posse on his tail
over the getaway sand
and logs the tide spat out like pips
into the joyous distance
nearly capsizing a little old lady
to sniff the newfound parts
of her imperious poodle

It's a pleasure of a morning
to watch him tumble and romp
savouring his moment
like a bone

Skeletons

After they found his twin brother's bones
the boy assumed the Cain mark—
the Crown stayed the proceedings
but he walked ever after
in a wind of accusing whispers
unable to tell the truth
about the protected father
who sat drunk and mad
in a cabin full of bottles
rotten socks   unopened mail
crushed under the weight
of the double guilt

When they discovered the woman
pilled to the eyes
she was cooking her old man's breakfast
"Oley will be getting hungry" she said
but Oley would never know hunger again
he was in the bed with the blood
and three more mouths than he was born with
in his back
"He fell against the knife" she said
so they set her free
and she drank herself dead

Now in this damp November
a friend has fallen prey
to a new act of violence
blown away forever
by the barrel of a maniac's gun
his familiar laughter
shattering like glass
against the brick wall of his death

Outside in the cold darkness
the dogs follow false trails—
the cops ride shotgun on the docks
roadblock the getaway routes
but their quarry is already long gone
It is Remembrance Day—
a man has remembered how to kill

The moon weaves fog like a yellow spider
around the stunned bar
where no one dances tonight
and the beer he will never taste again tastes bitter

Another backcountry bloodletting—
soon it will recede into legend—
be consigned to the town's closet
with all the rest of them
Do not be decieved by its picture-pretty face
this deceptive place
has hidden its full quota
of skeletons

There Are Many Ways

Sawclatter in the clearing—
sundust glittering on the leaves—
whiteblue brilliance aching in the eye of spring
this essential day of wood-gathering

This day reaching back fifteen years
to far less willing wood chores
grumbled over in the gritty dilemmas of then—
hamstrung with hopelessness—
foggy with false directions

No inkling in my hobbled mind
that the path would come full circle
through obscure woodchopping rituals
in the odd-job city basements
of drab destitute times
to this magic day, fraught with warm significance—
gladly swinging my axe for her—
burning the soft-life fats
at the forbidden altar of her nearness

Now it is too dark to work—
the wood is split and stored—
the evening fire crackles   the kettle sings—
I sit behind the smoke with pitch on my fingers—
there are many ways of expressing love

What the Wind Knew

No one in those pioneer shacks
those jerrybuilt bunkhouses
those tents and boatholds
those long houses on the longago dew,
could dream in arduous morning
their backs to the endless timber—
the green wall that walked forever,
what would ensue

No one foresaw it but the wind
crying its warning down the channels
moaning like an unheeded prophet
over the untrammelled land
No one listened but the trees
waiting silent for their downfall—
knowing time would soon betray them—
only they could understand

For the interlopers would multiply
in the crannies of the clean country
changes come beyond all reckoning
and the fat cities rise—
birds beside oil-clotted waters
bid a last farewell to flight—
perish with glued feathers
under smoke-haunted skies

The wind pawed the threatened edges
of the invaded continent
shrilling in the sure knowledge
of those ill-omens coming real
crying vainly in the untouched places
of the inevitable disasters—
of the wounds in the strongholds of perfection
that would never heal

The Abandonment

They crossed a wind-shaken sea
in a time before record or memory
to this edge-of-the-world island
where dwarf deer throng the moss-hung clearings
colossal forests comb the clouds
swift rivers sing the salmon home to die
Here they made landfall
took root like the ruling trees
harvested the fruitful woods and ocean
prospered and grew strong
named their adopted country
Gaawa Hanas—the enchanted place

Tales of their prowess
echo through legend
with forty-warrior canoes
they terrorized the mainland tribes
and in the contemplative time
gave substance to their gods in yielding cedar
Hook-beaked, the thunderbird hunched into being
the bear deity glowered
the wolf spirit bared wooden fangs
the whale god grimaced
Axe, adze, and knife
worried free the stark images
crude pigments stained them fierce
believing hands raised them
like towering icons
beside the busy villages
against the imponderable skies

The Abandonment

They crossed a wind-shaken sea
in a time before record or memory
to this edge-of-the-world island
where dwarf deer throng the moss-hung clearings
colossal forests comb the clouds
swift rivers sing the salmon home to die
Here they made landfall
took root like the ruling trees
harvested the fruitful woods and ocean
prospered and grew strong
named their adopted country
Gaawa Hanas—the enchanted place

Tales of their prowess
echo through legend
with forty-warrior canoes
they terrorized the mainland tribes
and in the contemplative time
gave substance to their gods in yielding cedar
Hook-beaked, the thunderbird hunched into being
the bear deity glowered
the wolf spirit bared wooden fangs
the whale god grimaced
Axe, adze, and knife
worried free the stark images
crude pigments stained them fierce
believing hands raised them
like towering icons
beside the busy villages
against the imponderable skies

Thus it was
through the cycles of uncounted seasons
until the outlanders came
in great winged canoes
smelling of tar and gunpowder
speaking in bewildering alien tongues
carrying beads   steel blades   bad rum
and bibles
to enlighten the heathen savages
misappropriate their land
disrupt forever
the delicate checks and balances
revile and condemn
the simple animistic beliefs

And from more than half a world away
they bore a deadlier cargo
The smallpox epidemics
spread like unseen fire
no spell   no fetish   no shaman's wiles
could halt their ruthless course
The lodges stank of death
the beaches were corpse-strewn
contagion raged
the Coast became a charnel ground

The owl called many names in that grim time
till the Haida lay near decimated
bad medicine had come to Gaawa Hanas
the villages were strange with wailing and silence

When the plague stayed its rampage
only one in ten remained alive
the stunned survivors
turned their backs on the cursed clearings
of the blighted homeland
paddled north to resettle on the higher island
leaving hollow lodges to the spirits of the lost

So it has been now for more than a hundred summers
in the untrammelled forests of Gaawa Hanas
where crumbling villages
still lift grey remains from the undergrowth
and rain-bleached totems gape wanly yet
It is one of the last strongholds of natural order
on all the scarred man-ravaged Coast
The curse that came upon the Haida here
was not of the land's making
It is still Gaawa Hanas—the enchanted place

Kitimat Floor Show

In that bar big as a football field
the players are getting restless
a gang of antsy ironworkers
voices wrangling   rising   challenging

"You lying sonofabitch!"
a table tips   glasses shatter
picking partners like hockey players
two dozen rowdies reel and clash

Three conscientious objectors
trapped in the vortex of the donnybrook
scramble over the partition
to the neutral zone of the Ladies side

Wrestling   cursing, the brawlers lurch wildly
through blind measures of mayhem
till the summoned cops come storming in
like a squad of gun-toting linesmen

Outside the battlezone
Big Gord Bastien, Jimmy Fiddle and me
watch as the dust settles
and the scrappers are hustled off to the hoosegow

"Floor show's over" grunts Big Gord
We order more beer   go back to being bored

Mohawk Jimmy

They never stilled
the killer in Mohawk Jimmy
after the blackface commando raids
the knives in the night
Battle was his natural element—
he thrived in the crash of combat
"I come from a long line
of oldtime warriors" he said

Mohawk Jimmy walked the smelter
with unrepentant Nazis
long after the war
swearing he recognized
the hated faces of old foes
with his coveralls like a dirty uniform—
swinging a gun that fired only grease—
leashed by peace

Then, one night in a bar,
liquor unleashed him once more
He went at the three Germans
with undiminished efficiency
When it was over, one of them
lay dead with a broken neck
The judge called it manslaughter
They sent him away to prison

They never stilled
the killer in Mohawk Jimmy
"I come from a long line
of oldtime warriors" he said

Thin Edge

That hard winter, the world
backed me into a corner   the wind
whined and agonized
down the Kitimat Valley   the wound
in my soul throbbed and festered

Fifteen-foot snow drifts
walled the road to the smelter
where we swing-shifted endlessly
through the fuming potlines
breathing smoke   coughing black dust

Stumbling blindly back and forth
between the job and the pub
with no saner future in sight,
I was trapped in a web of frozen futility—
hamstrung with hopelessness

One drunken night, the depressing truth
of my hollow existence closed in—
there seemed only one escape route—
the bottom dropped out of my common sense—
the top came off the pill bottle

Three dozen caps began to dissolve in my gut—
reality started to blur and dwindle—
shrank to a dot of white zero
like the pinpoint of light on a dying t.v. screen—
sprang back briefly   began to diminish again

I knew when that glowing dot blinked out
my life would blink out with it—
suicidal urge flashed to blind panic—
suddenly I didn't want to die
staggering to the medicine cabinet
I gulped half a bottle of emetic—
vomited up the undissolved pills
Gradually
the overdose slackened its grip—
reality reestablished itself—
the death dot was gone

Next day I returned to the smelter
with a brand new philosophy
the molten aluminum still bubbled and spat—
the great cranes rumbled overhead—
the pots stretched in lines like great smoking tombs—
somehow they seemed like old friends

Winter would pass—
I would pass too from the grimy inferno in time—
meanwhile I accepted my lot
I had learned beyond a doubt
that even this sort of life
is a damn sight better
than no life at all

Provisioning for a Journey
in memory of Doug Mackay

It was a though you were provisioning for a journey—
on every one of your final visists you borrowed more books
and we talked a lot about the past   those yesterday people
when life stretched out endlessly   into the blue illusion of morning

We touched those long ago days with yearning fingers of memory—
our youth-selves moved through them like faint ghosts—
the town sang back to its simple beginnings—
cows roamed freely once more those lost-to-glory streets

And there we were laughing at dirty jokes
on early cigarette afternoons
in all the sadhappy broken promise of our youth
time like a shielding wall holding the future at bay

But now the future has taken us prisoner—
time's shielding wall is pock-marked and crumbling—
things we can barely conceive of are waiting just around the bend—
we are caught in the current of the great invisible river

And now, my dear old friend, you have embarked
on that last lone journey you were provisioning for
with books and talk and things too soon to be taken back—
you have gone forever into the wind and the wonder

Inklings

Inklings

Death you're the persistent knocker
on doors of laughter and budding leaves—
you're innocence incarnate   the bare backside of the sun—
you're the Injun Joe in old caves

Death, you're the drafty window no one ever closes—
you're the unstoppable punchline to the world's oldest joke—
you're the reason stones don't crawl   they know better—
you're the dawn that won't break

Death, you're the unwritten song that is always sung—
you're the unwanted statement that is always made—
you're the rhythm beating beyond the broken drum—
you're the seductive hitchhiker thumbing our best road

Death, you threw my father from the bright sky and broke him—
you drowned my stepfather in the river of the lost abyss—
you peer through the china figures on my mother's mantlepiece—
you're the killer in the kiss

Death, you're quite unmoved by any reasonable objections—
you're the one contest we all reluctantly win—
you're the makeup man applying greasepaint in the mirror—
you're the poisonous pigment in my pen

Death, you're the cobra coiled in the joy—
you're the ever-boiling kettle and we're the fish—
you're the sharp-eyed doorman who spots the cleverest gatecrasher—
you're the stale soap melting in the dish

Death, you're a crafty cardsharp who cheats with cased aces—
you're the hurricane plotting mayhem behind the calm blue sea—
you're the message a child writes on the wall before he learns the
weary symbols—
you're me.

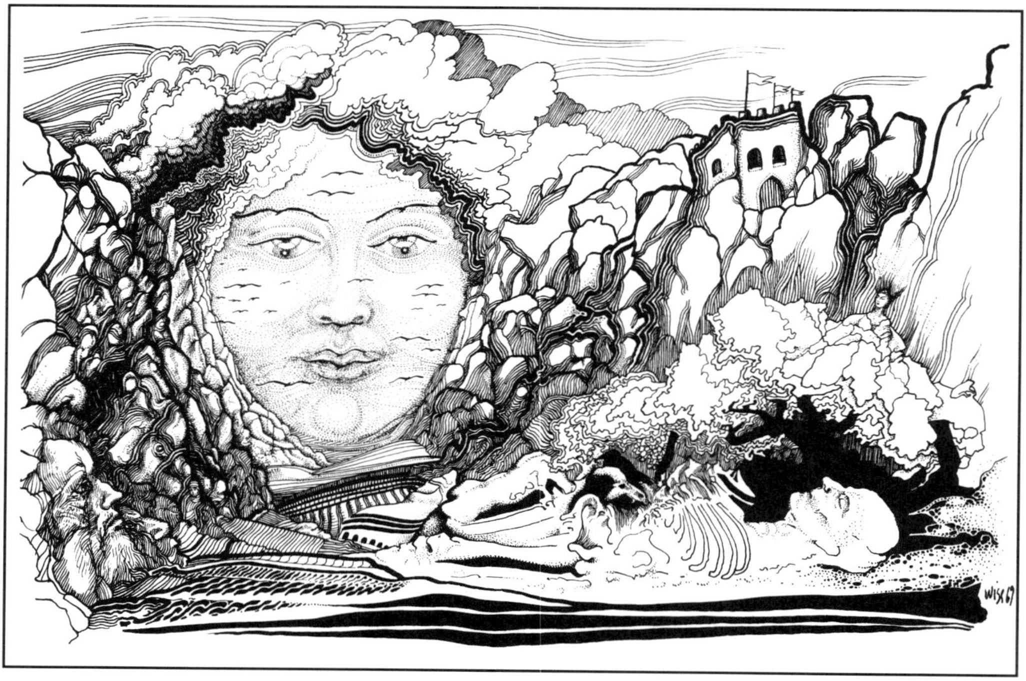
WISX 67

The Blasted Zone

Beneath bone skies
the doomstruck country stretches—
a waste of stillborn dreams—
betrayed illusions—
of gutshot hopes
and terminal confusions—
above that ruined land
the sad face watches

The sad face turns—
the social words are spoken—
the empty games resume—
the mask is smiling—
it hides a deathscape
where the skies are falling—
the lips move glibly
but the eyes are broken

Darks and Lights

There is no way to plot the odd delights
or all the sullen vacuums in between
we are the substance of our darks and lights

We seesaw from the nadirs to the heights
till death and neutral darkness intervene
there is no way to plot the odd delights

We feed the grief that tragedy invites
till joy comes slipping strangely through the screen
we are the substance of our darks and lights

The lack of love may agonize our nights
the luck of love may teach us what we mean
there is no way to plot the odd delights

We are the givers and the parasites
we reap the consequences as we glean
we are the substance of our darks and lights

In this rigged game, the wrongs will spawn the rights
the rights, the wrongs   the fruitful years, the lean
there is no way to plot the odd delights
we are the substance of our darks and lights

Arctic Air Front

North Pole cold
bullies out of the barrens
laying cowls of wet snow
on false-spring flowers   flaying
the night with knives of wind   winter
is stalking this sun-spoilt land again
taking it
by the scruff of the neck
shaking it
into new submission

Flung back into frigidity
by icicle fingers
clawing down from the Barrens,
we turn up the thermostats
jam another log in the heater
don sweaters   crouch
before coloured boxes watching
torched oil wells gouting flame and smoke
roads lined with mangled trucks   corpses
scattered like charred cordwood
cities shattered
by a grinding armada of air power
dictators blustering   generals
generalizing
in the name of the Pentagon   President Bush
and God
world-away War winding down
as the wind rises
whinnies and weeps

But these northern gusts
carry only cold—
their desert brothers
the siroccos   the simoons
bear the grimy pall from the blazing oil wells
a poisonous black fog of human folly
across the planet's face.

Prisons

Men with faces like cracked toby jugs
lurching past the mind—
frayed lustreless women
seeing bright hair   smooth skin
through straw-coloured glasses—
dark bar denizens
diligently blotting out reality

Once I saw a bird
fly bewildered
into just such a groggy enclave

How deftly he evaded
the tipsy grasping fingers
bobbed desperately
beyond their clumsiness
dipped   sideslipped   twitched—
beat terrified wings
against the ghost barrier
of the bar mirror—
in desperate frenzy
buzzed the crowd again—
caromed off the ceiling—
found at last
the bright rectangle of escape—
fled twittering relief
into the natural sun

Birds instinctively
know their proper place—
build no prisons

Humans
victimized by their wits and thirsts
are another matter

How many times
we find the exit doors too late—
sit addled beyond hope
hearing faintly through the muffling walls
the pure sound of the universe
going about its business sensibly beyond us

Goodbye to the South

Continental drift of clouds
moves against the slow roll of the world
across a storm-stropped sky
Flagcloth of the past
you are trailing torn allegiances—
the vestiges of all we were—
ragged banners shredding away
into figments and fragments—
empires of lost significance—
the lowest slave supplicating—
the first hesitant dauber on cave walls—
the hopeful women begetting cretins—
the sunquake of creation that fractured space—
God uncertain in heaven

In the timeless counrty of thought
a galley prow carves the water—
books and witches burn—
the voices of ignorance babble and gibber—
the voices of reason beg to be heard—
purposeless wars are declared and fought—
countries are crushed underfoot
in a bedlam of bombdust and blood—
nothing is resolved—
less is learned—
scholars ponder the perversity of it all—
children squander the money of their innocence—
the uncaring sun leaps and sinks—
stung by the lifefever, we stumble and twitch
down endless roads of false direction

What we were meant to be
still calls from an unsundered land
past all hazard or hint
Like dumbstruck robots
we march to thickening winters
imperceptibly slowing as we proceed
At last we stumble to a halt   our faces
fixed on the Northern lights   Our voices
stilled forever, we statue the lifeless wastes
of hope's blackfrost periphery
and it's goodbye to the South.

Decimal Street

Decimal Street
where the rules were kept
ran straight as a theorem
under the sky
mathematicians
hemmed and hawed
structuring minds
as time marched by

Dutiful students
heeded their words
recited their tables
tackled their sums
But some of us dozed
through classroom days
hearing the beat
of different drums

Then manholes opened
under out feet
We groped through sewers
to find the light
Equations became
a distant drone
as we bid goodbye
to Decimal Street

Unwanted algebra
bled from our brains
In strange new learning
stranger men taught
Numbers gave way
to instinct and luck
in the alternate schools
where truth is wrought

Now the poetry
sings to our touch
Deep in the past
the dull sums bleat
We have found a more random
arithmetic
We have broken the bonds
of Decimal Street

The Falling Away

The tree ruffles its feathers like a bird
in suburbia   The game's over—
a dance that was doomed before it began
I am thinking of love falling away

Nothing dies quicker than heady delusion—
it flames on blue days   then falls away
I watch wet laundry dance in the wind
I drink red bloody wine and think of you

You are gone beyond my foolish deceits
caught in the pull of your own needs and trades
The mountains rear far and cold in the distance
cynically white as wedding cakes

It's a gusty good day, I suppose
for weatherwatchers and little old ladies
but somewhere within me the rain falls hard
and where you laughed is a rift in reality

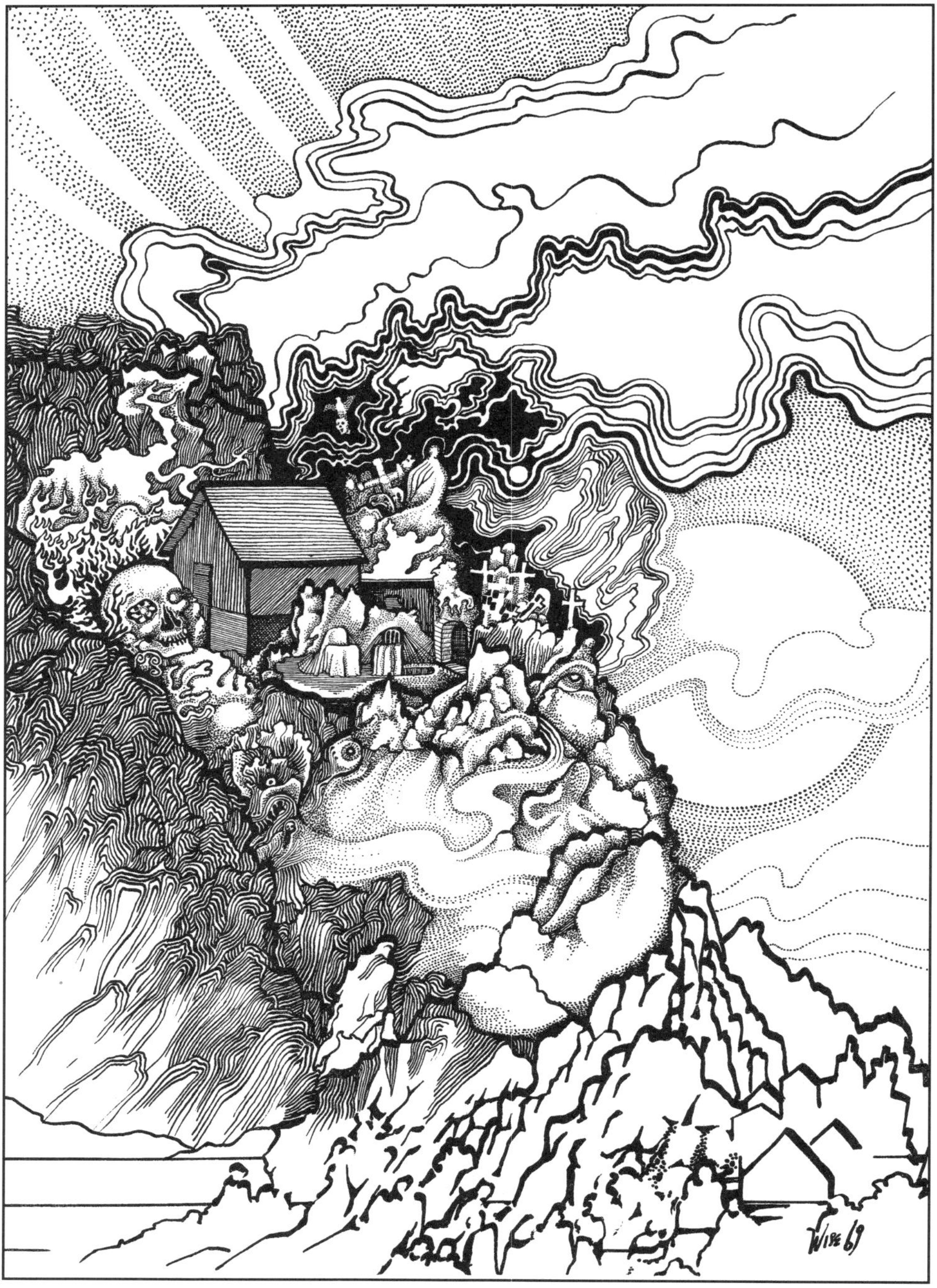
Wise 69

The Defector

I shall have no more affairs
with ghosts in crumbling cottages
to the echo of voiceless laughter
the conversations of chairs
watched from inhabited mirrors
by shadows that cannot rest
before the emberless hearthstones
on rugs of muttering dust

I shall whisper no more endearments
to earless listening skulls
beside the gravestoned gardens
where fingers grope from the soil
when the moon gapes mad from the sky
on midnights of gelid flame
striking the pits alive—
the lurkers locked in the clay

I shall bid farewell to my phantoms
my consorts of empty rooms
kiss no more the spectral lips
nor stroke the bodiless limbs
From these hills of other-than-life
I shall venture the crooked road
to the smug and unsupecting towns
haunted by flesh and blood

Mars Probe

A single drop of blood clinging
to an invisible black finger
you pulse scarlet light
in the bottomless pit of space
taking your closest look at us
for four decades
perhaps not liking what you see
in our cloudy crystal ball

Beacon of archaic warriors
scion of unnumbered sticky swords
martial star
livid liege of battle
reduced to a thin-sheathed ghost-globe
a moonpocked face
staring coldly at us   an estranged
threadbare brother
forged in common fury
when the sun spat worlds like pebbles

Our electronic emissaries
slide through void towards you
hungry for your sparse secrets
clicking out like metal insects
a barrage of electronic data
to cut the throat of myth
disprove the canals
vapourize fanciful conjecture

But there are no probes that can reach
that other Mars of our dreams
its ruined cities filled
with alien revelations
Red rides the lonely
its fantasies untrammelled
beyond unimaginative computers
in the brain's brighter gulfs

We Who Evade

You have come close sometimes
We have observed your diligent searchers
from screened vantage points
anticipated their movements
from obscure slopes

We are old and few now
who threaded this land
in the simpler time—
who feathered our lairs
under elysiumlight
before your kind evolved

Then we were many
in the world's quieter morning
moving at will
through unbroken forest—
the first ones

But we are a timid species
fearing the fire
in your hands and eyes
you the inquisitive ones
who rose to conquest
from a simian crouch
who glimpsed us fleetingly
named us troll   ogre
giant   yeti   sasquatch—
who harried us back
to the hopeless snowheights
the dim untravelled valleys

We are dying into time
and the stricken wilderness
one weary jump ahead
of your deadly curiosity
Grant us a quiet passing
we are only primeval echoes
Your true beastman   as always
snarls at you from the looking glass

The Day the Seas Went

The day the seas went
in one fell gurgle
for some obscure cosmic reason
of which I am not apprised
there were suddenly a billion acres
never before exposed
slimy pristine landscapes
new empires of squirming ooze

When the bottom fell out
of the Baltic   Atlantic   Pacific
there arose to the shocked skies
an overpowering stench
Seabirds suddenly sea-robbed
wheeled bewildered above great gulfs
It was raining krakens and whales
in the Mindanao Trench

Atlantis and Lemuria
lay at long last revealed
plus several other sunken lands
even legend had forgotten
but they were soon redrowned
in a downpour of fishy flesh
mist roiled to the stars
the depths were no longer hidden

From the awesome heights of the continents
the beaches gazed on abyss—
beyond the viscid expanses
the lowered horizon loomed
On dizzying mountain summits
the southsea islands perched
surrounded by dripping voids
where no surf drummed

It was a very curious business
all those boats and liners plunging
through the aquatic vacuum
into the miles-deep pits
but then   unfortunately
with the sudden pressure-release
internal fires
erupted through the crust in numerous places
the furious earth revolted
blew the whole surreal underscape
to bits

Mansion
in memory of Shirley Grauer

Through a mist of dream, the mansion
rises mutated—
not the actual place I once knew
where the wealthy widow
who was briefly my patron
introduced me to Bullshots
handed me cheques
and bought me a hairpiece,
but some surreal distortion
of that luxurious home
empty now, a nest
of nagging recollections

Somehow I seem to be staying
in the abandoned mansion
which is undergoing
a curious renovation—
anonymous workmen clump unseeing by me—
we do not speak

Wistfully I move
through the empty gutted rooms
envisioning what was
in halcyon years before my time
when an immigrant farmer's son rose to fame
created a power company
built this sprawling pile
raised a sprawling family here

All that's gone now, the mansion
is in the throes of change
I climb to the third floor
find a padlocked door
that opens to my touch
upon an enormous ballroom
far too huge for the building to contain
with other rooms unveiling themselves beyond

Perplexed, I descend again
to the ground floor
where the silent carpenters
are transforming this place into something
I don't want to know about

The dream begins to fragment   I fall
back towards
whatever reality is

The mansion behind me sinks
into a dark tarn of skewed memory
like the House of Usher.

Sifting the Debris

I am sifting the debris of several lifetimes
in this sold shell of a house
this womb of memories and crumbling wood
where I have coiled like a foetus
for too many years

Ghosts of old songs   lost circumstances
drift through the room like winter breath
I have breathed smoke and sorrow here
laughter too   confused love
of girls who were mostly mistakes
and one who wasn't—
of a small loyal mother
who killed me with kindness
raised me to poems
and vanished forever—
of brothers who burned by the wayside
and climbed from their ashes—
of friends, also brothers,
who bootstrapped to betterment   of friends
who put guns in their mouths
jumped from bridges and windows
walked up lonely valleys with noosed ropes
passed like sad echoes

Phantom cats
lie curled on window ledges of recollection
like mongrel shades they haunt
this sagging mansion of other days—
from incomprehensible distances
their trusting paws reach out
their small voices speak to me yet

This house where once I retied
a psychic umbilical cord
and made a shaky pact
with alcohol and words,
reaches out beyond me into time
each invisible finger
a conduit to another yesterday
all the yesterdays before my birth—
my mother safe in Malayan girlhood—
my father biplaning over the Himalayas—
my learned grandfather deciphering Greek in his study—
my practical grandmother tending her kitchen and gardens

And all the forebears before them
indistinct legends
dwindling into history

I am sifting the detritus
of much more than myself
in this dusty focal point
where a long phase is stumbling
to a final halt—
an obscure epoch
stuttering into silence

I relinquish custody
of this museum house and its relics—
collapsed portal to the past—
rotted afterbirth of dreams.

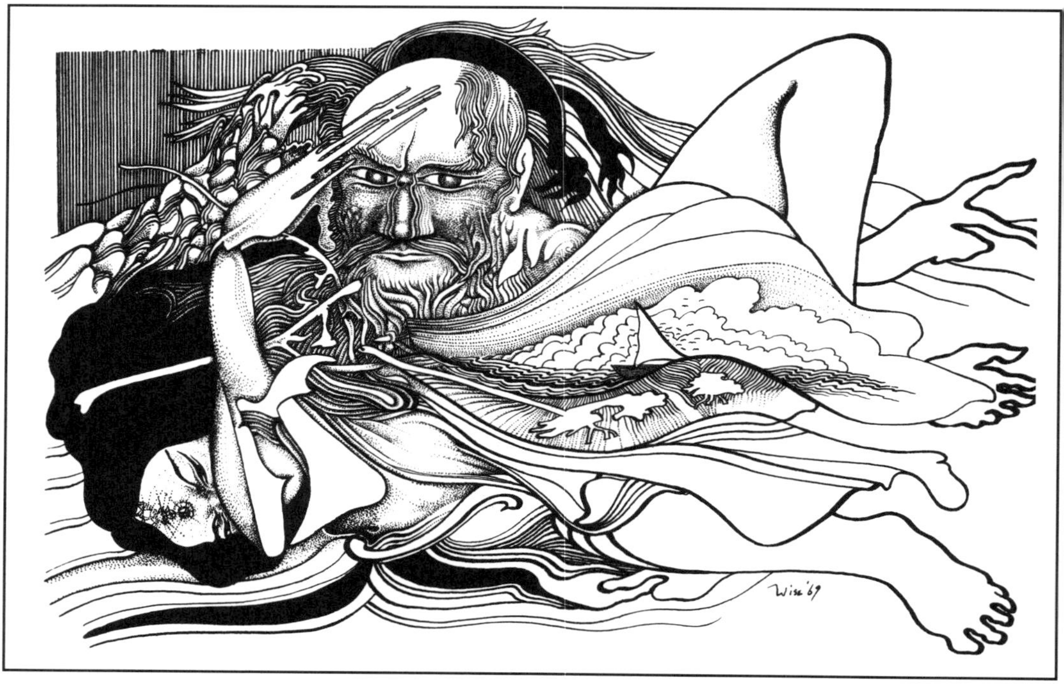
Wise '69

My Thoughts Swim After You
for Yvonne

As you drift away from me up the Coast
into adventures I cannot share
I yearn for the song of you
that magicked me into a whole person
when we laughed together
on the best days I have ever known

There was a strain in our parting—
a painful edgy awkwardness
it cuts me to recall—
words turned inadequate—
a stiff and bitter silence
dropped between us

On this warm uncertain afternoon
my thoughts swim after you
as you journey northward—
my ghost hand caresses your hair—
my ghost mouth brushes your lips—
my ghost arms close around you

Once, years ago, you moved away from me
down the windy reaches of Long Beach
before I had learned to walk with you
Then you returned and began to teach me
all the special secrets of your being
It was the first real lesson of my life

Come back to me again, my darling
along that profounder beach
that is the rest of our lives
You are my only true companion—
my love beyond all other loves
We have walked the weathers
hand in hand
I have forgotten
how to walk alone.

On Uncharted Seas
in memory of my friend, Stuart Nutter

There is no orderly way
out of this mortal riddle—
we are seldom packed and ready
on that last decisive day

Trailing loose ends
we are pulled willy-nilly from the game
full of unspoken last words—
leaving the useless grief of friends

Into light's last arabesque
we dance dully—
there are clean socks in the drawer—
a final letter lies forever unfinished
on the cold desk

The blunt facts are these—
death is a mischievous boy
waiting to cut our tow ropes—
to set the boats of us adrift
on uncharted seas

Sweet Daddy in the Dark
for Stuart Nutter

My old gentleman friend
I address you too late
from this side of the curtain
that has dropped forever
on your dreams and pains

Now in the unfathomable dark
may you meet your mother   my mother
my father   your father
in realms beyond alcohol
in realms beyond agony

Let all the things that might have happened for you
happen gladly now in some unimagined place
Drift and be happy
in endless and ethereal joy
where all is wise   complete and final

Say farewell to your friends   your family
staggered   saddened by your passing
Bless their coming
Bless their gathering
Bless the gentle way we sent you over

There is nothing left here but us
who blunder on through clockwork folly
Watch us kindly now and smile
old brother
old confidante
old companion
sweet daddy in the dark

Millennium

Seventy years beyond my birth
I open the gates of old age
and consider the convoluted road
that has brought me to them
in a world where technology
has quantum-leapt forward
into the internetted future
while political philosophy
seems to be inexorably backtracking
into the meanhearted past
as we enter a new millenium
in a daze of dichotomy and confusion

Had I ordered my days differently—
not drunk so many of them away
along with the nights   I might
be sitting in happier circumstances
with less lost opportunities
tugging at my conscience—
fewer guilty memories
of the many people
I have failed and disappointed
through self-obsessed thoughtlessness—
blind misunderstanding—
inexcusable neglect

Looking back on a haphazard life
I see reluctantly
a scattering of unfortunate events
for which I can feel only honest regret
There is no way to alter these negative facts—
they are part and parcel of what I was   and am—
I must carry them with me
like a chafing burden

down unknown pathways
to the end of this bewildering journey
buoyed also by the many good and glowing things
that far outnumber the bad
for after all those lonely years I loved   was loved
and that was both a gift and a glory.

Remembering Al
A tribute to Al Purdy

Hey, Al
I remember an afternoon in the late Sixties
before we became friends
you and Milt Acorn, poets in full flight
storming into the Cecil pub   following your cigars
like a couple of rumpled Groucho Marxes
to set up shop at a corner table
ordering beer   continuing some arcane argument
while another nonentity and myself sat looking on
mightily impressed

And that prophetic meeting in 1972
you were so fond of recounting
when, along with Howie White and Curt Lang,
consuming humungous quantities of beer
then descending on a startled Esther Birney—
Earle being out of town—
regaling her with steaks, more beer and poetry
till the poor lady's head must have been spinning
like the possessed girl's in *The Exorcist*

Four years later in Toronto
at the launch of *Storm Warning 2*
where you'd managed to bypass the under-30 age-limit
by including my stuff in the intro—
you were in fine fettle that night
playing King of the Poets with obvious gusto
while lonely Milton scribbled obliviously in a back room—
turning to me, you said, one arm around the McStew p.r. lady,
"All this could be yours someday, Pete
if you just keep on writing" —
I wish you'd been right but, come to think of it,
that p.r. lady was way too tall for me anyhow

And the first time we read together
at the Literary Storefront in Gastown
you and Eurithe just back from Mexico
with suntans and new poems—
me only three days away from my mother's impending death
trying not to dwell on it—
you and Eurithe suitably sympathetic—
you and I doing our respective things—
late to the Cecil with George Bowering,
Andy Suknaski and a slew of others
for a bout of drunken poetic blather

Sechelt Writer's Festival, several years after this—
Yvonne and I, finally together, picking you up at the seaplane dock
you sporting a new moustache   very impressed by Yvonne—
down to my late mother's house for beer and talk—
me showing you my first mimeographed collection of jingly doggerel—
you remarking charitably that is wasn't as bad as *The Enchanted Echo*—
you asking how the writing was going—
me, just rejected by McStew, saying "Not too great" —
you offering to edit and agent the manuscript for me—
taking it east with you   placing it with Oberon—
God knows, Al, that was a decent thing for you to do—
you gave me my confidence back

And the years and the years and the years

Sidney in the Nineties and our only serious quarrel—
triggered by your Roderick Haig Brown book *Couger Hunter*—
you figuring I had somehow doublecrossed you—
writing me a peevish, accusatory letter to that effect—
me firing one right back to set things straight—
the matter, thankfully, ending right there—
God knows, Al, I owed you too much to ever sell you out

And then the treacherous cancer   the inexorable decline—
you phoning me from Ameliasburgh to tell me that Peggy Atwood
was revising her Oxford anthology and to send my best poems
still being my dutch uncle even in your exigency—
me asking nervously about your condition—
you saying you'd finished the radiation but hadn't got the results—
me saying wishfully: "Hell, Al, you're tough. You can beat this" —
you saying wistfully, realistically: "Afraid I'm not that tough" —
and sadly, of course, you weren't

Our last meeting—Yvonne and I dropping in
to give you a copy of *Chainsaws in the Cathedral*
the book you had always been after me to put together—
for which you had both coined the title
and written the great introduction—
you thin and frail but still in good spirits, looking pleased
urging me, as always to keep on writing—
me thinking I was glad to be able to give it to you
while you were still around—
it was as though we had completed a project
embarked upon a long time ago

Hey, Al
I guess you're maybe sitting in a rented room
on one of the outer planets by now
writing new poems we'll never get to read
or perhaps you're strolling the hills and valleys
of legendary Gondwanaland, a billion years ago—
be well, old friend, wherever you are in unfathomable eternity—
unlike the title of your final book you will never be
Beyond Remembering

Through the Apricot Air

A poet is dreamfooted and walks a curious tightrope—
his song rises strangely through the apricot air—
love is his joy   his tool   his wisdom   his folly—
he circles mothlike the candleflame truth of things

He strikes from nothing the sparks of what ought to exist—
the knowledge aches out of his eyes   creation's his purpose—
he scrawls on the sky   inhabits the lunatic corners—
in the web of delusion he crouches, alert as a spider

A poet is a decoder of arcane messages—
received on the crystal set of his eavesdropping heart—
from the scrabble-bag of letters he plucks the singing images—
threads them like beads on the lines of his secret longing

He is a cardsharp of words that sting and praise and wonder—
his mind swings erratically between micro and macrocosm—
he studies the eccentric comings and goings of house finches
and the ghostly pillars that whelp stars at the edge of the universe

A poet is a brief mad seer in a sea of bottomless mysteries—
he is driven more by curiosity than wisdom—
he lives his life by luck, intuition and chance
and leaves as his legacy only a random scattering
of delirious verse.

The Pause

Cessation rules a kingdom of the halted
between a moment and its beating sequel—
the licences of breath have been suspended—
the quick of all the world are frozen equal
The sun stands pat in the sedated heavens—
the clouds hang anchored and the wind is balanced
like a stunned bird above the static landscape
while birds lie painted on the china silence

The green machinery beneath the fields
has struck its flag and stopped the sap from flowing
The cogs of trees   the mainsprings of the grasses
have ceased their secret work and turn no growing
The panting midnight lover's nailed naked
The crafty leopard's pasted to his jungle
The sprinter's foot is poised above the cinders
The mole's plugged like a bullet in his tunnel

It is the interlude   the time of no time
and somewhere and away, the comet's feathers
are pinned between the worlds that whirl no longer
and cataleptic stars, their fury tethered
It is the pause   the terrible hiatus—
the patient waits for statues to dissect him
In every vastness   every atom's essence
the sound of motion's strangled like a victim

And only now, beyond the great abeyance
a sad and monolithic figure paces
To be or not to be?   To quit or quiver
He walks alone and weighs enormous choices
"I'll try it once again"   He spreads his fingers
"Perhaps this time I may achieve the vision"
The universe resumes its dream of process
to flicker on until the next decision.

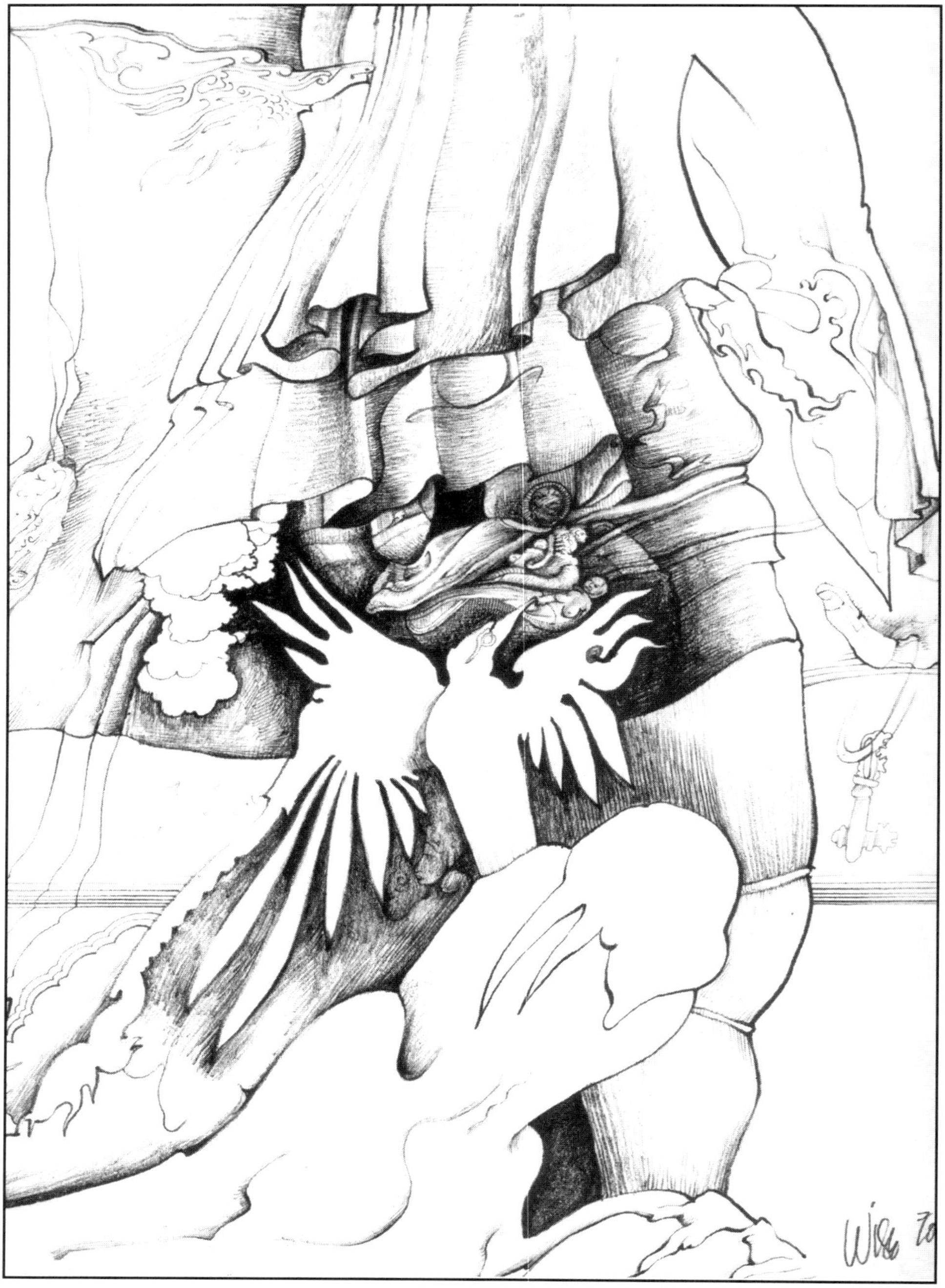

About the Author

Peter Trower worked as a logger for twenty years and is the author of nine books of poetry and three novels: *Grogan's Café*, a novel of West Coast logging life; *Dead Man's Ticket*, a mystery with a similar setting; and *The Judas Hills*, published by Harbour publishing. His articles and poems have appeared in a variety of periodicals. He has also appeared as himself in the TV movie *The Diary of Evelyn Lau*. Peter Trower's collection of logging poems *Chainsaws in the Cathedral: Collected Woods Poems* was selected for the B.C. 2000 Millenium Award. In 2002 he was awarded the B.C. Gas Lifetime Achievement Award for his work. He lives in Gibson's, B.C.

About the Artist

Jack Wise was born on April 27, 1928 in Centerville, Iowa. He completed a Bachelor of Fine Arts degree at Washington University, St. Louis. In 1955, Wise received a Master of Science in Art degree done at Florida State University. He emigrated to British Columbia in the 1960s, and began homesteading in the B.C. interior. With his wife, Mary, Jack had three children in the early seventies. After several years living between various homes in Victoria and on islands off the coast of Vancouver Island, Wise moved to a cabin on Denman Island for the final years of his life. Surrounded by nature and secluded in his home, Wise was able to meditate and paint uninterrupted. His art often takes images from the natural surroundings of the Pacific Northwest and other inspiration considered to be Western, and approaches them with a technique based upon the strokes of Chinese calligraphy. He left an immense and impressive body of work that is rooted in his great spiritual education and understanding. Jack Wise died at the age of 68 in November of 1996.